Pebbles, Sand, and Silt

Developed at
Lawrence Hall of Science
University of California at Berkeley

Published and Distributed by **Delta Education**

ISBN 10: 1-58356-831-X
ISBN 13: 978-1-58356-831-6
542-2034

7 8 9 10 11 12 QUE 12 11 10 09 08 07

Table of Contents

Exploring Rocks

Think about a rock. What does the
rock look like? Rocks can be small
or large. They can be smooth or
rough. They can be round or flat,
shiny or dull. Rocks can be different
in many ways.

Some rocks are too big to hold in your hand. A rock can be as big as a mountain!

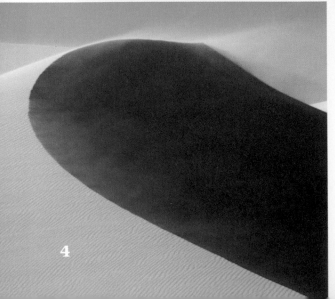

Other rocks are so small that you can hold thousands in your hand. Look at the picture of a sand dune. Can you see the tiny rocks blowing in the wind?

4

Rocks of all sizes can be found in rivers.
Over time, rocks in a river become smooth.
Rocks become smooth from rubbing
against one another.

Rocks of all sizes can
be found in a desert,
too.

How big is the rock
you're thinking of?

Rocks can be many colors. They can be black, brown, red, or white. They might even be pink or green. Some rocks have speckles or stripes, too.

Rocks can be many different sizes. They can be many colors and shapes. They can even have patterns.

What does the rock you're thinking about look like?

Colorful Rocks

What are these colorful objects?

The answer is minerals. There are many different kinds of minerals. And minerals come in lots of different colors.

Rocks are made out of minerals. That's why rocks can be so many different colors.

This rock is made of at least three different minerals. Can you see them?

Look for the black mineral.

Look for the pink mineral.

Look for the gray mineral.

These are the minerals in this rock.
This rock is called granite.

The Story of Sand

Have you ever looked at one grain of
sand and thought . . . "I wonder how
it got so small?"

A grain of sand wasn't
always so small!
It may have once
been a boulder.
The boulder could
have broken off.
It could have tumbled
down the mountain.

Perhaps the boulder rolled into a river.
Water in a river can move rocks.
The rocks bump together in the water.
The boulder might have broken into cobbles
and pebbles. Cobbles are bigger than pebbles.

Maybe the river carried the pebbles
to the ocean. The ocean waves crashed
over the pebbles. The pebbles may have
broken into gravel. Gravel is smaller
than pebbles.

ver time, they
maller. They can
ocks. These tiny
nd.

sand castle,
of sand!

Rocks Move

Water and wind move rocks of all sizes.

Look at the pictures on these two pages.
Can you tell what moved the rocks?

Washout

Sandy Beach

Mudflat

15

Making Things with Rocks

People use rock to make things. A quarry is a place where people dig rock out of the earth.

Big pieces of rock are used to make
big things. Statues and churches are
often made from rock. People make
things out of rock because it is strong.

Smaller rocks are useful, too. Rocks are part of the mixture that is used to pave streets.

Gravel and sand are often used to make sidewalks. The gravel and sand are mixed together with cement. Cement is like glue. It holds the mixture together.

Even the tiniest rocks arc useful. Clay is made up of rocks that are tinier than sand! They are so small that it is hard to see only one rock. People mold clay into many shapes.

Whatever their size, rocks are useful. People use them to make strong and beautiful things.

What Is in Soil?

Rocks are all around you. The soil
under your feet has rocks in it. Some
of the tiny rocks in soil are called silt.
Silt is smaller than sand, but bigger
than clay. Sand, clay, gravel, and pebbles
can be in soil, too.

When plants and animals die, they become part of the soil. Plants and animals decay into tiny pieces called humus. Humus provides nutrients for plants. It also helps the soil hold water.

What is this animal that lives in soil?
A worm! Worms are good for soil.
They burrow through the soil. They
break it apart and eat the humus.
Worms help plants grow by mixing
and turning the soil.

Not all soil is alike. Some soil
has more humus. Some has
more clay or sand. Some has
more pebbles and gravel. What
differences do you see in these soils?

Testing Soil

Do plants grow better in soil or sand?
Here's what some students did to find out.

1. They used cups that were all the
   same size.
2. They filled some cups with potting
   soil that had lots of humus. They
   filled the other cups with sand.
3. They planted a few sunflower
   seeds in each cup.
4. They put the same amount of
   water in each cup.
5. They kept the cups in a sunny window.

Think about it!

Do you think these students thought of a good way to test the question?

Which seeds grew better? Why do you think that happened?

What would you have done to record what happened each day?

How should they report the results of their test?

Fossils

How do we know what Earth looked like millions of years ago? We look at fossils. Fossils are parts of plants and animals that turned to rock a long time ago. Scientists study fossils to learn about the past.

Dinosaurs lived a long, long time ago. No dinosaurs are alive today. But scientists can study dinosaur fossils to learn about them.

One of the most famous dinosaur fossils is named Sue. Sue is a *Tyrannosaurus rex*. This is what Sue looked like when she was found in South Dakota.

Scientists dug
Sue out of
the ground
very carefully.

In the lab, Sue's
fossil bones were
carefully cleaned.

After a lot of hard work, all of
Sue's bones and teeth were ready
to put together.

It took a long time to get all the
fossil bones in the right places.
Finally, the bones all fit together.
Everyone can now see what Sue's
skeleton looked like.

After the skeleton was together,
scientists wanted to know what Sue
looked like when she was alive. They
put muscles, skin, and eyes on a copy
of her skeleton to make her look real.

This is what Sue might have looked like.

Glossary

Cement - a finely ground powder that sets and hardens when mixed with water.

Decay - when dead plants or animals break down into small pieces.

Fossil - a part of a plant or animal that lived long ago and has turned to rock.

Humus - bits of dead plant and animal parts in the soil.

Minerals - the ingredients that make up rocks.

Nutrients - something that living things need to grow and stay healthy.

Rock - a solid earth material. People who use rocks for making things sort them by size. The names of the different rock sizes (from largest to smallest) are

- **Boulder** (rocks 10 inches across or larger)
- **Cobble**
- **Pebble**
- **Gravel**
- **Sand**
- **Silt**
- **Clay** (rocks so small it is hard to see just one)